BASEBALL LEGENDS

Hank Aaron
Grover Cleveland Alexander
Ernie Banks
Johnny Bench
Yogi Berra
Roy Campanella
Roberto Clemente
Ty Cobb
Dizzy Dean
Joe DiMaggio
Bob Feller
Jimmie Foxx
Lou Gehrig
Bob Gibson
Rogers Hornsby
Reggie Jackson
Shoeless Joe Jackson
Walter Johnson
Sandy Koufax
Mickey Mantle
Christy Mathewson
Willie Mays
Stan Musial
Satchel Paige
Brooks Robinson
Frank Robinson
Jackie Robinson
Pete Rose
Babe Ruth
Nolan Ryan
Mike Schmidt
Tom Seaver
Duke Snider
Warren Spahn
Willie Stargell
Casey Stengel
Honus Wagner
Ted Williams
Carl Yastrzemski
Cy Young

NEWFIELD
PUBLICATIONS

BASEBALL LEGENDS

CARL YASTRZEMSKI

Shepard Long

Introduction by
Jim Murray

Senior Consultant
Earl Weaver

CHELSEA HOUSE PUBLISHERS
New York • Philadelphia

Published by arrangement with
Chelsea House Publishers.
Newfield Publications is a federally
registered trademark of Newfield
Publications, Inc.

CHELSEA HOUSE PUBLISHERS

Editorial Director: Richard Rennert
Executive Managing Editor: Karyn Gullen Browne
Copy Chief: Philip Koslow
Picture Editor: Adrian G. Allen
Art Director: Nora Wertz
Manufacturing Director: Gerald Levine
Systems Manager: Lindsey Ottman
Production Coordinator: Marie Claire Cebrián-Ume

Staff for CARL YASTRZEMSKI

Assistant Editor: David Carter
Designer: Diana Blume
Picture Researcher: Alan Gottlieb
Cover Illustration: Daniel O'Leary
Editorial Assistant: Laura Petermann

Library of Congress Cataloging-in-Publication Data
Long, Shep.
Carl Yastrzemski/Shep Long.
p. cm.—(Baseball legends)
Includes bibliographical references and index.
Summary: A career biography of one of baseball's great fielders, Carl Yastrzemski.
ISBN 0-7910-1195-X
0-7910-1229-8 (pbk.)
1. Yastrzemski, Carl—Juvenile literature. 2. Baseball players—United States—Biography—Juvenile
literature. 3. Boston Red Sox (Baseball team)—Juvenile literature. [1.Yastrzemski, Carl. 2. Baseball
players.] I. Title. II. Series.
GV865.Y35L66 1992
796.357'092—dc20
[B]

91-40219
CIP
AC

CONTENTS

WHAT MAKES A STAR

Jim Murray

No one has ever been able to explain to me the mysterious alchemy that makes one man a .350 hitter and another player, more or less identical in physical makeup, hard put to hit .200. You look at an Al Kaline, who played with the Detroit Tigers from 1953 to 1974. He was pale, stringy, almost poetic-looking. He always seemed to be struggling against a bad case of mononucleosis. But with a bat in his hands, he was King Kong. During his career, he hit 399 home runs, rapped out 3,007 hits, and compiled a .297 batting average.

Form isn't the reason. The first time anybody saw Roberto Clemente step into the batter's box for the Pittsburgh Pirates, the best guess was that Clemente would be back in Double A ball in a week. He had one foot in the bucket and held his bat at an awkward angle—he looked as though he couldn't hit an outside pitch. A lot of other ballplayers may have had a better-looking stance. Yet they never led the National League in hitting in four different years, the way Clemente did.

Not every ballplayer is born with the ability to hit a curveball. Nor is exceptional hand-eye coordination the key to heavy hitting. Big-league locker rooms are filled with players who have all the attributes, save one: discipline. Every baseball man can tell you a story about a pitcher who throws a ball faster than anyone has ever seen but who has no control on or *off* the field.

The Hall of Fame is full of people who transformed themselves into great ballplayers by working at the sport, by studying the game, and making sacrifices. They're overachievers—and winners. If you want to find them, just watch the World Series. Or simply read about New York Yankee great Lou Gehrig; Ted Williams, "the Splendid Splinter" of the Boston Red Sox; or the Dodgers' strikeout king Sandy Koufax.

A pitcher *should* be able to win a lot of ballgames with a 98-miles-per-hour fastball. But what about the pitcher who wins 20 games a year with a fastball so slow that you can catch it with your teeth? Bob Feller of the Cleveland Indians got into the Hall of Fame with a blazing fastball that glowed in the dark. National League star Grover Cleveland Alexander got there with a pitch that took considerably longer to reach the plate; but when it did arrive, the pitch was exactly where Alexander wanted it to be—and the last place the batter expected it to be.

There are probably more players with exceptional ability who didn't make it to the major leagues than there are who did. A number of great hitters, bored with fielding practice, had to be dropped from their team because their home-run production didn't make up for their lapses in the field. And then there are players like Brooks Robinson of the Baltimore Orioles, who made himself into a human vacuum cleaner at third base because he knew that working hard to become an expert fielder would win him a job in the big leagues.

A star is not something that flashes through the sky. That's a comet. Or a meteor. A star is something you can steer ships by. It stays in place and gives off a steady glow; it is fixed, permanent. A star works at being a star.

And that's how you tell a star in baseball. He shows up night after night and takes pride in how brightly he shines. He's Willie Mays running so hard his hat keeps falling off; Ty Cobb sliding to stretch a single into a double; Lou Gehrig, after being fooled in his first two at-bats, belting the next pitch off the light tower because he's taken the time to study the pitcher. Stars never take themselves for granted. That's why they're stars.

1

THE IMPOSSIBLE DREAM

On Sunday, October 1, 1967, Boston's Fenway Park was filled to capacity for the final game of the regular season between the Boston Red Sox and the Minnesota Twins. During the preceding month, baseball fans across the country had witnessed one of the most exciting pennant races in American League history. No fewer than four different teams had taken turns in first place.

Now, with just one day remaining in the season, the Red Sox and the Twins were tied for first place with identical 91–70 records; the Detroit Tigers were only half a game behind, at 90–70. Unless the Tigers took both games of their doubleheader against the California Angels that afternoon, the winner of the Red Sox–Twins game would become the American League champions.

For the Red Sox and their fans, just being in a pennant race was a miracle in itself. Boston had finished ninth in the 10-team league the previous season. And the ballclub had not won an American League title in 21 years.

Soon to be named the American League's most valuable player in 1967, Carl Yastrzemski stands ready to pace the Boston Red Sox' pursuit of the pennant, a chase that lasted until the final day of the season.

In April 1967, the Red Sox were considered 100–1 longshots to win the pennant. And even as late as the All-Star break, they were in fifth place, a mere two games above .500.

But somehow this team of underdogs persevered. And on the final day of the regular season, Boston was just one win away from a trip to the World Series. Their amazing quest for the pennant had even taken on a name of its own. It was called the Impossible Dream.

The 1967 Boston Red Sox was a team of overachievers. But there was one player who stood out above the rest, who seemed capable of making the Impossible Dream come true all by himself. His name was Carl Yastrzemski, but hardly anybody called the 27-year-old outfielder by his full name. To baseball fans across New England, he was just plain Yaz. And in 1967 he could do no wrong.

The year marked Yastrzemski's seventh season in the major leagues but the first in which he lived up to expectations of being an all-around superstar. In years past, he had established himself as a fine hitter and an excellent fielder, but in the summer of 1967 he blossomed as a power hitter as well. Whenever the Red Sox needed a timely base hit or a clutch home run, a diving catch or a game-saving throw, Yaz delivered it. In fact, just one day earlier, he had clubbed his 44th home run of the season, a three-run shot that had helped Boston beat Minnesota, 6–4, and move back into a first-place tie.

A standing-room-only crowd packed Fenway Park the next afternoon to see if Yastrzemski and the Red Sox could come through one more time. The Twins were leading 1–0 in the third

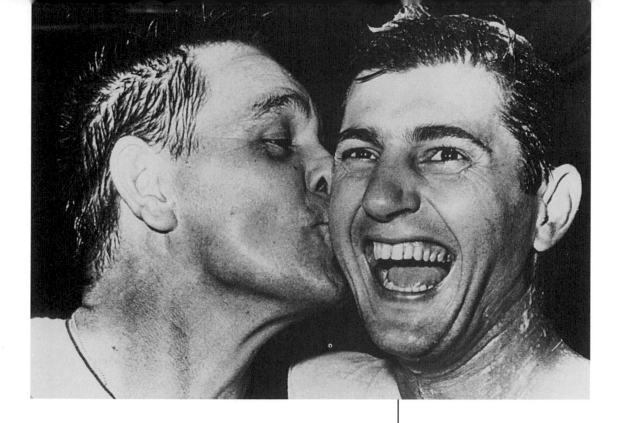

inning and had a runner on first base when Harmon Killebrew lined a single to left field. Yastrzemski charged the ball aggressively, hoping to hold the base runner at second base. Instead, he let it skip under his glove for an error, and the runner raced all the way around the bases to score.

It was only Yastrzemski's seventh error of the season, but the miscue could not have come at a worse time. Dean Chance, the ace of the Twins staff, was pitching for Minnesota. He had already won 20 games during the season, including a no-hitter, and could make a 2–0 lead seem very large indeed.

Yastrzemski singled and doubled in his first two at-bats against Chance, but the Red Sox failed to score, and the game remained 2–0 when Boston batted in the sixth inning. Three straight singles loaded the bases with no outs,

Red Sox manager Dick Williams (left) plants a kiss on Yastrzemski's cheek in the Boston locker room after their ballclub beat the Minnesota Twins, 5–3, to clinch at least a tie for the 1967 American League pennant.

bringing Yastrzemski to the plate for his most important at-bat of the season. "I was so anxious to hit, I practically ran up to the plate," he recalled. "I was never more sure of myself in my life." As Yastrzemski listened to the crowd's cheers, he was tempted to swing for a home run. Then he thought better of it. Instead of taking the chance of overswinging, he concentrated on making solid contact. He wound up lashing a single to center field for his third hit of the afternoon; it drove home two runs and tied the game. By the time the inning was over, Yastrzemski had also come around to score, and the Red Sox owned a 5–2 lead.

The score remained unchanged until the Twins mounted a rally of their own in the eighth inning. With two out and two runners on base, Bob Allison ripped a line drive down the third-base line for what looked like a sure double; a two-bagger would score two runs and put the next Twins batter in position to tie the game. Yastrzemski was off with the crack of Allison's bat and backhanded the base hit before it could roll into the left-field corner. Then Yaz whirled and unleashed a perfect throw to second baseman Mike Andrews. Allison tried to slide, but to no avail. He was out, the inning was over, and Boston still had the lead.

One inning later, Minnesota's Rich Rollins popped out to end the game, touching off a wild celebration at Fenway Park. The Red Sox rushed to congratulate winning pitcher Jim Lonborg as fans poured onto the field from all directions.

But the pennant race was not over quite yet. The Tigers had captured the first game of their doubleheader. And if they won the second game as well, they would tie Boston for first place and force a one-game playoff for the pennant on Monday. So the Red Sox gathered in the locker room, where they listened to the second Tigers-Angels game on the radio.

As they waited for the outcome, Boston manager Dick Williams congratulated his star player. "Thanks, Yaz," the team's skipper said. "You had a fantastic season."

In fact, Yastrzemski had put together one of the finest seasons in baseball history. He had just become the eighth American Leaguer ever to win the Triple Crown, topping the junior circuit in batting average (.326), home runs (44), and runs batted in (121). He had also led the league in hits, runs scored, total bases, and slugging percentage. And he would win a Gold Glove for his outstanding play in the field.

Perhaps most impressive of all, in the last 12 games of the season, when the pressure was greatest, Yastrzemski had batted an amazing .523 with 5 home runs, 14 runs scored, and 16 runs batted in. In the final two must-win games against the Twins, he had collected seven hits in eight at-bats.

In Detroit, the Tigers took an early 3–1 lead, then fell behind and trailed 8–5 as they batted in the bottom of the ninth inning. The Red Sox listened nervously as Detroit put runners on first and second, bringing the tying run to the plate with no outs. But Jim Price flied out, and Dick McAuliffe grounded into a game-ending double play, kicking off another wild celebration back in Boston, this time in the locker room.

The 100–1 Red Sox had won the American League pennant. Thanks in large part to Carl Yastrzemski's brilliant season, the Impossible Dream had come true.

2

YASTRZEMSKI TO YASTRZEMSKI

Carl Michael Yastrzemski was born on August 22, 1939, in Southampton, New York, a small, rural town on the eastern end of Long Island. Southampton was about 100 miles from New York City and seemed even farther than that. Carl's parents, Carl, Sr., and Hattie, were part of a large Polish community, and they made their living as potato farmers, just as their ancestors had done in Poland for centuries.

There was always plenty of work to be done on the Yastrzemski farm. And as soon as Carl, Jr., was old enough, he was expected to do his share. In the summer, he often awoke at five in the morning and worked from dawn until dusk filling sacks of potatoes and then loading them onto a truck. In the winter, when there was no crop to be harvested, he spent hour after hour cutting the eyes out of potatoes for planting the following spring.

Between the backbreaking work of harvesting potatoes and the tedium of cutting them, Carl had other jobs to do. He worked in the family's backyard garden, where the Yastrzemskis

Yastrzemski celebrated his final game as a high school ballplayer by pitching a no-hitter and striking out 18 of the 21 batters he faced to nail down the Suffolk County B Class baseball championship for Bridgehampton.

Bridgehampton Wins Crown for Third Year; Yastrzemski Shines, Faces 21, Fans 18

Young Carl Yastrzemski said goodbye to high school sports last Monday in a blaze of glory, when he pitched a no-hitter against Center Moriches to win the B Class baseball championship for the Bridgehampton high school, 1-0, at neutral Westhampton.

It was a performance that will go down in the records as one of the greatest exhibitions in school sports in this, and probably in a much larger, area. It allowed the small Bridgehampton school to win, for the third year in a row, the B Class championship, and gave that magician, coach Merle Wiggin, something to write in his book of memories.

Carl faced twenty-one batters and struck out eighteen of them. Only three balls were hit. One was a high hopper to third that

CARL YASTRZEMSKI
Carl is holding the Quimby trophy, won by the school at the game. A replica was given to him.

Outstanding Athlete Goes to Notre Dame

Carl Michael Yastrzemski, who last Monday made history in Weshampton when he no-hit Centre Moriches to win the B Class flag for Bridgehampton

grew all their own food. The Yastrzemskis also made their own butter, and Carl spent many hours at the butter churn.

Despite all the hours devoted to working on the family farm, Carl still found time for fun. Like most young boys, he enjoyed sports. And in the Yastrzemski family there was one sport that was almost as important as the daily chores: baseball.

Carl Yastrzemski, Sr., was an outstanding baseball player. A few years before Carl, Jr., was born, Carl, Sr., had been offered a minor league contract by the Brooklyn Dodgers. Unfortunately, the offer came during the mid-1930s, when America was mired in the Great Depression. Millions of people were unemployed; many more lived from day to day not knowing how long they would have a job.

Carl, Sr., was thrilled by the offer, but he also had a family to support. Staking his future on a career in baseball was too risky. He knew that as long as he stayed on the farm, he would have work and his family would have food to eat. Carl, Sr., decided he could not give that up, not even for a chance to play for the Dodgers. So he continued farming and also formed his own baseball team, the Bridgehampton White Eagles.

The White Eagles was a family baseball team. Every player was either a Yastrzemski or a Skonieczny, which was Carl's mother's maiden name. They were not the equal of a major league team, of course, but they held their own against the other amateur teams in the area.

Carl became the bat boy for the White Eagles almost as soon as he was big enough to hold a bat. After watching his father and uncles play baseball day after day, summer after summer, it was only natural that he would want to follow in their footsteps. Carl devised dozens of different drills to hone his baseball skills. Whenever he had a spare moment, he could be found swinging a bat or pitching against a wall that was marked with a chalk strike zone.

During his hitting drills, young Carl would often pretend to be one of his favorite major league players, usually Joe DiMaggio or Stan Musial. Carl liked DiMaggio because he was the star of the youngster's favorite team, the New York Yankees. Musial, who played for the St. Louis Cardinals, was like Carl: he was Polish and batted left-handed.

Carl's only brother, Rich, was four years younger than the future Boston Red Sox star, so when Carl wanted to bat against "live" pitching he often turned to his uncles on the White

Eagles. Competing against older players who were much bigger and stronger than Carl made him even better. By the time he was 12, none of his uncles could strike him out.

Carl starred on the Bridgehampton Lions Little League team as a shortstop and pitcher. With Carl as their leader, the Lions made it to the state finals.

When Carl turned 15, his father let him join the White Eagles. For Carl, Sr., playing baseball alongside his son was as big a thrill as playing for the Dodgers would have been. But many of their teammates on the White Eagles could no longer keep up with the younger players on the other teams, and the ballclub soon had to fold.

With the end of the White Eagles, the two Carl Yastrzemskis joined a semiprofessional team, the Lake Ronkonkoma Cardinals. The Cardinals paid them $20 each per game. Even though Lake Ronkonkoma was 60 miles from Bridgehampton, the Yastrzemskis made the trip three times a week to play against the best possible competition.

Carl, Jr., played shortstop and batted third, while Carl, Sr., played second base and batted fourth. For the Lake Ronkonkoma team, "Yastrzemski to Yastrzemski" proved to be a potent double-play combination.

But Carl, Jr., was becoming more than just an outstanding young baseball player. He was blossoming into a splendid all-around athlete, playing football and basketball in addition to baseball at Bridgehampton High School.

On the football field, Carl played quarterback—or at least he did until his senior year, when his father forbade him to play. Carl, Sr., was afraid his son might injure himself and ruin a chance at a professional baseball career. Carl, Sr., had missed his own opportunity to play for the Dodgers years ago, and he was determined not to let a similar thing happen to his son.

In spite of his father's ban, young Carl secretly went out for the team. When his father found out, Carl, Sr., literally dragged his son off the practice field, bringing a dramatic end to Carl, Jr.'s, football career.

Carl, Jr., was upset when he was not allowed to play football anymore, but he could still play basketball, which he liked almost as much as baseball. In fact, he practiced his outside shooting almost as diligently as his batting. Carl was not particularly tall (he was barely six feet) or fast, but by his senior year he had become a fantastic shooter. He scored 47 points in one game, 46 in another, and averaged a whopping 34 points per game. His scoring average set a Suffolk County record that lasted for three decades.

But Carl's first love remained baseball. At Bridgehampton High School, he played shortstop and pitched, just as he had in Little League. Carl's talent did not go unnoticed. During his senior year, scouts from several major league clubs watched him closely.

In the semifinals of the 1957 Suffolk County high school baseball tournament, Carl pitched a two-hitter against Bellport, striking out 16 batters. Three days later, Bridgehampton played Center Moriches for the county championship, and Carl was even better. He pitched a no-hitter and struck out 18 batters.

The next day, the New York Yankees called Carl and asked him to come to Yankee Stadium for a tryout.

*While attending The University of Notre Dame,
Yastrzemski continued to work on such baseball funda-
mentals as laying down a bunt.*

3

BONUS BABY

The New York Yankees were clearly the best team in baseball while Carl Yastrzemski was growing up. In the 17 years between his birth and his tryout with the ballclub, the Yankees had won 11 American League pennants and 10 world championships. They were easily his favorite team, and for young Carl a highlight of each summer was going with his father to Yankee Stadium to see Yogi Berra, Whitey Ford, Mickey Mantle, and the rest of the Bronx Bombers storm to another title.

In 1957, when Carl, Jr., arrived at Yankee Stadium for his tryout, ballclubs did not take turns picking the high school and college players they wanted in a draft. Every team had the right to sign an athlete so long as he had finished high school. A top prospect usually received a huge bonus just for signing, which meant that if he had enough talent, he could become rich overnight.

A player who was handsomely rewarded was called a bonus baby, and Carl, Sr., felt his son deserved to be one. The teenager's performance during his tryout at Yankee Stadium did nothing to change his father's mind. Carl, Sr., watched his son take batting practice before a game against the Cleveland Indians. Carl, Jr., was given just 10 pitches to hit, and he belted 4 of them into the seats. That was all the Yankees brass needed to see. They did not even ask him to pitch or play the field.

Lee MacPhail, the Yankees general manager, promptly sat down with the two Yastrzemskis to negotiate a contract. New York offered a $40,000 signing bonus, and young Carl was ecstatic. Not only was that more money than anyone in his family had ever seen, but he would also be getting a chance to play for his favorite team.

Carl, Jr., could not believe his ears when his father said no. "It's more money than we've ever offered to a high school kid before," MacPhail insisted. But Carl, Sr., had made up his mind. No team was going to sign his son for less than $100,000, not even the mighty New York Yankees.

Later that week, the Yankees sent a scout, Ray Garland, to the Yastrzemski house to raise the bonus to $60,000. But Carl, Sr., would not budge. Instead, he suggested that his son consider going to college. Carl, Jr., had already received hundreds of scholarship offers for both baseball and basketball.

At the end of the summer, 18-year-old Carl Yastrzemski took his father's advice and enrolled at the University of Notre Dame on a half-baseball, half-basketball scholarship. But the teenager quickly became discouraged there. College freshmen were not allowed to play on the varsity sports teams, so all he could do was practice.

One day during batting practice, Yastrzemski belted a ball more than 500 feet from home plate. It landed on the football team's practice field. Hank Stram, who later coached the Kansas City Chiefs to the Super Bowl, was an assistant coach for the Fighting Irish at the time, and when the ball came flying onto the field he said, "I'll bet Yastrzemski hit this."

In the spring of 1958, when Yastrzemski returned to Bridgehampton after his freshman year, he discovered that the major league scouts had not forgotten him. The Los Angeles Dodgers and the San Francisco Giants both offered him contracts. But his father did not want his son

Yastrzemski takes a practice swing at the Red Sox training camp in 1960. Although he was determined to make the ballclub's roster that spring, he was sent to Boston's top farm team, the Minneapolis Millers of the American Association, to be converted into an outfielder.

playing so far away from home. Another team interested in the young ballplayer was the Philadelphia Phillies. Yastrzemski was so impressive in his Phillies tryout that they increased the bonus ante to $95,000. So eager were the Phillies to have Yastrzemski join their club that they even offered him a spot that very night in the starting lineup against the Chicago Cubs. Still, the bonus they offered was $5,000 less than Carl's father wanted, and by September the teenager was headed back to Notre Dame.

When Thanksgiving vacation rolled around, Carl, Jr., was still unsigned. By then, however, he and his father had narrowed his choices down to three finalists: the Detroit Tigers, the Cincinnati Reds, and the Boston Red Sox.

The Reds actually offered the most money, but the Red Sox had two other factors in their favor. First, Boston's Fenway Park was only a six-hour drive from Bridgehampton, and Carl, Sr., wanted to be able to see his son play as often as possible. Second, Tom Yawkey, the Red Sox owner, had a reputation for treating his players very well throughout their careers.

When Boston offered Yastrzemski a $108,000 signing bonus, a two-year minor league contract, and the rest of his college tuition paid in full, he signed. At long last, he was a professional baseball player.

Yastrzemski returned to Notre Dame to finish the fall semester, but he did not re-enroll after the Christmas break. He reported instead to spring training with the Red Sox, then journeyed south to join the Raleigh (North Carolina) Caps in the Carolina League for his first season of professional baseball.

Yastrzemski started off slowly with the Caps. But a visit by his father straightened out Carl, Jr., and he ended the 1959 season with a .377 average, the best in the league. He also paced the Carolina League in hits (170) and doubles (34), while socking 15 home runs and driving in 100 runs.

Shuttled between shortstop and second base, Yastrzemski made a league-high 45 errors. But his poor fielding did not detract from his fantastic season at the plate. He was named the Carolina League's most valuable player and picked up his first nickname as a professional ballplayer: Yastro.

4

"DON'T WORRY ABOUT BEING TED WILLIAMS"

Yastrzemski faced a pressure-packed season when he returned to the Red Sox spring training camp in 1961. In addition to replacing the Hall of Fame–bound Ted Williams in left field, he was being picked by the local sportswriters to win the American League's Rookie of the Year Award.

After his highly successful season with the Raleigh Caps, Carl Yastrzemski turned his attention to life outside of baseball. In January 1960, he married Carol Casper, a secretary from Pittsburgh whom he had met on a blind date while at Notre Dame. But before he could settle into married life, it was time to head for Florida and spring training.

Yastrzemski had attended the Boston Red Sox spring training camp in 1959 but had failed to make the big league squad. Now, in 1960, he already had a successful season as a professional under his belt. And with Boston coming off a fifth-place finish, he figured that if he played well during spring training, the Red Sox would have to find a place for him in the lineup.

Boston had rivaled Yastrzemski's beloved New York Yankees for supremacy in the American League during the late 1940s. The Red Sox fell upon tougher times in the 1950s, however, and never finished higher than third. Even so, the Boston lineup boasted the American League's premier attraction: the hard-hitting

Ted Williams. His talent was so extraordinary that many baseball experts considered the Red Sox left fielder to be the greatest hitter of all time.

By 1960, Williams was already a sure bet to become a Hall of Famer. He had captured nine slugging titles and six batting championships, two Triple Crowns and two MVP Awards. In 1941, he had batted at an astonishing .406 clip, making him the last player in history to reach the coveted .400 mark. He would retire second in lifetime slugging percentage (.634), third on the all-time home run list (with 521 home runs), and sixth in career batting average (.344).

By baseball standards, Williams was already a senior citizen in 1960; he would turn 42 before the end of the season. But he was still one of the most feared hitters in the league. And his locker at the Red Sox 1960 spring training camp was right next to Yastrzemski's.

The 20-year-old hopeful tried to learn about hitting from the veteran star. But when the two players talked, Yastrzemski felt Williams was speaking another language. Williams talked constantly about hip rotation and optimum swing angles; for him, batting was a science.

Ted Williams offers batting pointers to promising Red Sox hopefuls (from left to right) Jim Pagliaroni, Yastrzemski, and Bob Tillman in the spring of 1961. Half a year earlier, Williams had played his last game for Boston.

Yastrzemski tried to keep up with Williams's theories, but the only words that made a lasting impression were "Be quick" and "Study the pitcher."

Yastrzemski worked out at second base during spring training. And when the exhibition season began, he got off to a hot start, batting well over .350. But in the middle of training camp, he was sent down to the Red Sox' top farm club, the Minneapolis Millers of the American Association. He was shocked by the demotion, but he got an even bigger surprise when he arrived in Minneapolis. Gene Mauch, the Millers manager, was waiting for him. "We're switching you to left field," Mauch said. Yastrzemski was speechless. Not only had he never played the outfield before, but left field was Ted Williams's position. "Williams is going to retire after this season," Mauch explained, "and they want you for left field."

With the Boston organization grooming him to replace Williams, Yastrzemski enjoyed another great season in 1960. He batted .339 and led the American Association with 193 hits. He also put together a 30-game hitting streak. More important, he improved every day as an outfielder. When he finished the season, he had 18 assists and only 5 errors.

Yastrzemski understood that he would not be treated as an ordinary rookie when training camp opened in 1961. Still, he had no idea just how intense the pressure would be. Both the Associated Press and the *Sporting News* had made him their preseason choice to win the American League Rookie of the Year Award. Red Sox fans expected him to pick up right where Williams had left off.

Yastrzemski bolts across home plate to polish off an inside-the-park home run. Always a threat to sock an extra-base hit, he led the American League in homers once and in doubles three times.

The Boston management added to the pressure by giving Yastrzemski uniform number 8 instead of 44, which had been his number in the minors. The message to the rookie was very clear: Williams had worn number 9, and the Red Sox brass wanted Yastrzemski to be the next-best thing.

To make his situation even more difficult, many of the team's veterans resented both the attention Yastrzemski received from the press and the money he was making. His six-figure signing bonus had already netted him more money than some of the Red Sox had earned in their entire careers—and he had not even played in a single major league game! Some of his teammates began to call him Cash.

The Red Sox opened the 1961 season on April 11, playing against the Kansas City Athletics at Fenway Park. Yastrzemski singled in his first at-bat. Later in the game, he threw out a runner at home plate. Unfortunately, that day was one of the few highlights of his rookie year. By June, he was hitting only .220.

One day, after yet another hitless game, Yastrzemski sat by his locker, on the verge of tears. He was afraid that he would be sent back to the minors. Manager Mike Higgins came over and delivered a pep talk. "Don't worry about it," the manager said. "Don't worry about being Ted Williams or anybody else. Even if you hit .200, you're my left fielder every day." Yastrzemski hit near .300 for the rest of the season and finished the year at .266.

Most rookies would be thrilled to hit .266 with 11 home runs and 80 RBIs. But to the Boston fans, Yastrzemski's 1961 season was a flop. When Ted Williams was a rookie in 1939, he had hit .327 with 31 home runs and 145 RBIs. Obviously, Carl Yastrzemski was not the new Ted Williams.

Yastrzemski was not even the best rookie on the Red Sox. His teammate Don Schwall was 15–7 with a 3.22 ERA—numbers that were good enough for him to win the 1961 American League Rookie of the Year Award.

For Yastrzemski, the worst part of his first few seasons in the majors was dealing with the Boston fans. In Fenway Park, the stands along the third-base line extend almost to the foul line, then rise up into the left-field corner and meet the 37-foot-high wall known as the Green Monster. The fans in the corner, as well as in other parts of cozy Fenway, are virtually on top of the players. Every night Yastrzemski listened to them tell him how much better Williams had been. The abuse got so bad that Yastrzemski even wore cotton in his ears during one game.

The following year, Yastrzemski improved steadily and hit .296 with 19 home runs and 94 RBIs. He also led the league's outfielders in assists with 19. The next season, he made the American League All-Star Team for the first time, hit .321 to win his first American League batting championship, led the league in assists again (with 18), and won his first Gold Glove Award.

Unfortunately for Yastrzemski, the Red Sox teams he played on were not very good. In his first six seasons, their best finish came in 1961, when they wound up sixth. In 1966, Boston finished next-to-last for the second straight year.

Yastrzemski was getting tired of losing, and he promised himself that the 1967 season would be different.

Racing toward Fenway Park's monstrous left-field wall,
Yastrzemski makes a spectacular backhanded catch of
St. Louis Cardinals outfielder Curt Flood's line drive in
Game 1 of the 1967 World Series.

5

"YOU'RE GOING TO HAVE YOUR BEST YEAR"

Carl Yastrzemski began to prepare for the 1967 season almost as soon as the 1966 season ended. He had finally graduated from college, earning a bachelor of science degree from Merrimack College near Boston. (He had attended the school when it became impossible for him to return to Notre Dame at the end of each baseball season.) For the first time since high school, he could devote an entire winter to staying in shape.

Yastrzemski spent the winter of 1966 working out with a personal trainer named Gene Berde. The Red Sox left fielder sweated his way through a grueling six-day-a-week regimen of sprints, jump rope, weightlifting, and just about anything else Berde could think of. By the time spring training rolled around, Yastrzemski was in the best shape of his life. Gene Berde pronounced himself satisfied. "Yaz," he predicted, "you're going to have your best year ever."

Las Vegas bookmakers had made the Red Sox 100–1 longshots to win the American League pennant. Yet it was not hard to believe

Trainer Gene Berde (right) helps Yastrzemski get in shape for the start of another baseball season. "Yaz," Berde predicted correctly before the start of the 1967 campaign, "you're going to have your best year ever."

that 1967 might be the year that Boston finally escaped the bottom half of the standings. The team had a new manager, Dick Williams, who preached an aggressive, hustling style of play. Williams quietly surrounded Yastrzemski with an impressive array of talented young players. Tony Conigliaro, Jim Lonborg, Rico Petrocelli, George Scott, and Reggie Smith were all budding stars under the age of 25.

By the end of May, Yastrzemski was on his way to another fine season. He was hitting .299, but with more power than he had ever shown before. By early June, he already had 10 home runs and 31 RBIs. And the Red Sox were actually in third place. They were only four and a half games behind the Detroit Tigers and four behind the Chicago White Sox.

As Boston headed west to play Chicago in early June, White Sox manager Eddie Stanky made a grave tactical error. He got Yastrzemski mad. Stanky was quoted in a newspaper as saying that Yastrzemski was "an All-Star from the neck down." When the two teams met in a doubleheader later that week, Yastrzemski went six for nine, including a home run.

On July 11, Yastrzemski was the starting left fielder for the American League All-Star Team. The junior circuit lost the game, 2–1, in 15 innings, even though Yastrzemski reached base five times, on three hits and two walks. And each time he reached first base, he was congratulated by Stanky, who was coaching first base for the American League squad.

The surprising Red Sox remained close to the league leaders throughout the summer. Then, on August 17, tragedy struck. All-Star right fielder Tony Conigliaro was hit in the head with a pitch by California Angels fastballer Jack Hamilton. The beaning put Conigliaro in the hopsital and caused him to miss the rest of the season.

Yastrzemski took it upon himself to make up for Conigliaro's absence. He hit a sizzling .417 during the final month of the season, with 9 home runs and 26 RBIs. When the dust finally settled, he had won the Triple Crown, and Boston had won the pennant.

Gene Berde's preseason prediction had come true: Yastrzemski had enjoyed his finest season. His 44 home runs were more than double his best previous total and set a Red Sox record for left-handed batters; even Ted Williams had never hit more than 43.

The 1967 World Series pitted Boston against the St. Louis Cardinals, who had won 101 games in the National League. For the Red Sox,

Red Sox outfielder Tony Conigliaro is carried off the field on a stretcher after being knocked unconscious by a Jack Hamilton fastball on August 17, 1967, at Fenway Park. The beaning resulted in Boston's loss of Conigliaro for the season and seriously endangered the team's pennant hopes.

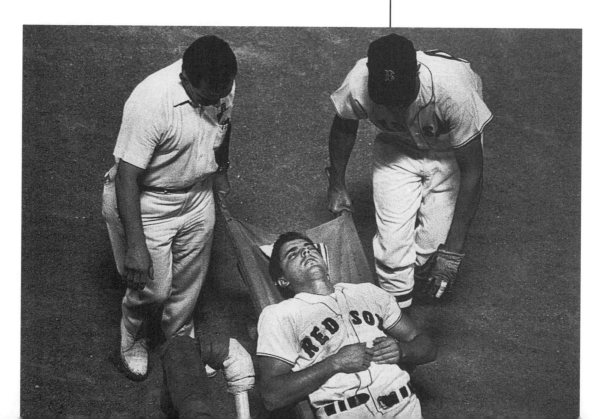

Yastrzemski launches one of his two home runs in Game 2 of the 1967 World Series to pace the attack in Boston's 5–0 white-wash of the St. Louis Cardinals. He also homered in Game 6 and finished the series with a .400 batting average.

having to compete in the Series was almost a let-down after such a stirring pennant race. Still, they played valiantly.

After losing the Series opener by the score of 2–1, Boston won Game 2 as Yastrzemski launched two home runs and Jim Lonborg retired the first 20 batters en route to one-hitting St. Louis, 5–0. The Cardinals then captured the next two contests to pull within a victory of the championship. But Lonborg posted a 3–1 triumph in Game 5, and Yastrzemski hit another homer in Game 6 to help Boston even the Series at three games apiece. St. Louis won the decisive seventh game, however, as the overpowering Bob Gibson picked up his third win of the 1967 Fall Classic.

Yastrzemski, who finished the Series with a lofty .400 batting average, was voted the American League's most valuable player. He was also named Sportsman of the Year by *Sports Illustrated* and edged Green Bay Packers quarterback Bart Starr for the Hickok Belt, which was awarded to the top professional athlete of the year.

After coming so close to a world championship with such a young team in 1967, the Red Sox looked like contenders for years to come. Instead, they found out how fleeting success can be. Conigliaro never fully recovered from his beaning, and Lonborg, the American League winner of the 1967 Cy Young Award, injured his knee in an off-season skiing accident.

In 1968, Boston slipped back to fourth place. Yastrzemski did his part, hitting .301 (which made him the only American League player to top the .300 mark) and winning his second consecutive batting championship. In 1969, when the Red Sox finished third, Yastrzemski reached the 40-homer, 100-RBI plateau for the second time in his career. He also made one of the greatest catches in All-Star Game history, leaping high and reaching above the outfield fence to rob Cincinnati Reds catcher Johnny Bench of a home run.

In the 1970 midsummer classic, Yastrzemski collected four hits to tie Joe Medwick's and Ted Williams's All-Star Game record and was named the contest's most valuable player. The 1970 regular season ended two and a half months later, with Boston again in third place, as Yastrzemski posted numbers that rivaled those from his Triple Crown season: he clubbed 40 home runs, scored a league-high 125 runs, drove in 102 runs, stole 23 bases, paced the circuit in slugging with a .592 average, and hit .329—the highest batting average of his career.

Alex Johnson of the California Angels, who also hit .329, wound up winning the 1970 batting title by .0003. Had Yastrzemski gotten just one more base hit, he would have earned his third batting crown in four years.

A familiar sight to Boston Red Sox fans: the left-handed Yastrzemski connects with a pitch at Fenway Park.

CAPTAIN CARL

Each season from 1967 to 1970, Carl Yastrzemski averaged 37 home runs, 106 runs, and 102 runs batted in. During that stretch, he was also one of the American League's best defensive outfielders. He won Gold Glove Awards in 1967, 1968, and 1969 despite having to patrol one of the trickiest places in all of baseball: left field in Fenway Park.

Most American League outfielders had nightmares about playing balls off Fenway Park's enormous left-field wall, with its uneven surface and unpredictable caroms. Yastrzemski, however, became a master of the Green Monster. Seeing the speed and spin of the baseball as it came off the bat, he could tell almost instantly not only where the ball would hit the wall but where it would land. He combined his knowledge of the wall with his outstanding athletic ability and powerful throwing arm, making opposing batters reluctant to try to stretch a single to left field into a double.

During his first decade with the Boston Red Sox, Yastrzemski also established himself as one

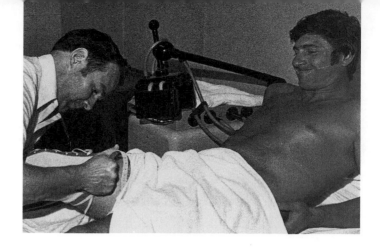

Yastrzemski grimaces in pain as his right knee is put into a brace by Red Sox trainer Buddy LeRoux. The Boston left fielder tore ligaments in the knee while sliding into home plate on May 9, 1972.

of baseball's most durable players. Although he occasionally suffered the nagging strains and sprains that plague all professional athletes, his minor injuries almost never stopped him from taking the field; he did not go on the disabled list once during his first 10 big league seasons. And from 1966 to 1970, he missed only 9 of 810 regular-season games.

In 1971, however, Yastrzemski was not so fortunate. The 32-year-old star sprained some ligaments in his wrist at midseason, and swinging a bat became so painful that he resorted to taping it directly to his hand to lessen the strain. He finished the season batting just .254, with only 15 home runs, none of which came after the injury.

The beginning of the 1972 season was even worse. In early May, Yastrzemski tore ligaments in his knee while sliding into home plate against the California Angels. The doctors suggested immediate surgery, but Yastrzemski chose rehabilitation instead. He was on the disabled list for a month before returning to the lineup in mid-June. He did not hit his first home run of the year until July 22. The same player who had been averaging nearly 40 home runs a season had suddenly gone almost a full calendar year without a single round-tripper.

"I had lost confidence in myself as a hitter," Yastrzemski admitted. He was playing so poorly that he even began to consider retiring. But then another pennant race came along, and once again Yastrzemski played like a living legend. Boston had not been in a true pennant race since the Impossible Dream season of 1967. And it seemed that Yastrzemski and his teammates would again be also-rans in 1972; by August 1, the ballclub had slipped to seven games out of first place in the American League's Eastern Division. (Both major leagues had split into two divisions in 1969.) They stormed back into contention by early September, however, with a rejuvenated Yastrzemski leading the way. He hit .306 with 8 home runs and 24 RBIs in the final six weeks of the season as the Red Sox dueled the Detroit Tigers for first place.

In 1972, a players' strike had forced the cancellation of the first week of the season. One result of the strike was that when the season finally began, not every team had the same number of games remaining on its schedule. Detroit, for example, was to play one more game than Boston, and that one game proved to be the difference between first and second place. The Tigers finished with an 86–70 record, edging the Red Sox, who ended the season at 85–70, by a half game in the standings.

Yastrzemski's sensational performance in September abruptly put an end to his own thoughts of retirement. The Boston public, however, continued to speculate that his age might finally be catching up to him. And who could blame them? Even with his strong finish, he hit just 12 home runs in 1972, his lowest total since his rookie year.

In 1973, the Red Sox moved Yastrzemski from the outfield to first base to protect his aging legs. He had played first base occasionally since 1968, but it was usually just to get a brief rest from the daily rigors of the outfield. He considered left field his true position, but in 1973 he found himself playing just 14 games there.

At the plate, Yastrzemski was still dangerous, even though he was no longer a Triple Crown threat. He hit .296 with 19 home runs and 95 RBIs in 1973. The following season, he hit .301 and led the league in runs scored with 93. He also drew more than 100 walks each year, an indication that the pitchers around the league still feared him and refused to throw him strikes.

Other than Yastrzemski, the 1975 Red Sox had only one other starting player from the Impossible Dream season left on their roster: Rico Petrocelli. Still, the two teams were quite similar in many ways. Like its 1967 counterpart, the 1975 club was loaded with emerging stars. Boston had 23-year-old Dwight Evans in right field, 24-year-old Rick Burleson at shortstop, and 26-year-old Carlton Fisk behind the plate. The ballclub also boasted what was perhaps the greatest rookie combination in baseball history in outfielders Fred Lynn and Jim Rice.

The biggest difference between the 1967 and 1975 teams was Yastrzemski's role. Where he had once been the star of the show, he was now just another supporting actor, although a very important one. Playing first base, he was the steady veteran who anchored the infield and to whom the younger players looked for leadership. And even though he disliked the title, his new

Sidelined because of a broken hand, Boston's powerful rookie slugger Jim Rice gazes wistfully at Cincinnati's Riverfront Stadium during the 1975 World Series. Rice's injury meant a return to left field for Yastrzemski, who had been moved from the outfield to first base back in 1973.

nickname, Captain Carl, was proof of the great respect he had earned.

At age 36, Yastrzemski put together a somewhat disappointing season (.269, 14 home runs). But Boston won the American League's 1975 Eastern Division title by relying heavily on the fabulous play of Lynn and Rice, who finished first and second, respectively, in the American League Rookie of the Year voting. Lynn, in fact, became the only player in baseball history to win the Rookie of the Year Award and Most Valuable Player Award in the same season.

In late September, the Red Sox' postseason hopes were dealt a severe blow. Rice, who had taken over Yastrzemski's post in left field, was hit by a pitch that broke his hand; he could not play again that season. Yastrzemski, who had only played eight games in the outfield during the regular season, was shifted to left field for the American League Championship Series against the mighty Oakland Athletics.

By 1975, Oakland was a baseball dynasty. The ballclub had won the World Series each of the previous three seasons, joining the New York Yankees as the only club ever to win three

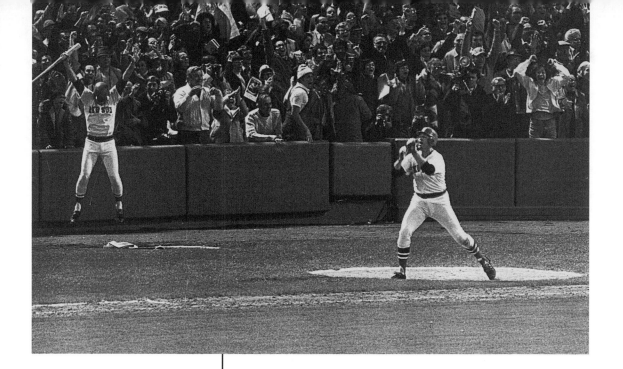

Red Sox outfielder Fred Lynn (left) jumps for joy as teammate Carlton Fisk (right) celebrates his dramatic 12th-inning home run, which gave Boston a 7–6 victory in Game 6 of the 1975 World Series. The contest has gone down in history as one of the most exciting ballgames ever played.

straight world championships. And with superstars such as Vida Blue, Rollie Fingers, and Reggie Jackson on the roster, the Athletics seemed a fair bet to make it four in a row.

Most observers expected Oakland to make short work of the upstart Red Sox in the American League Championship Series. Few, if any, people expected Yastrzemski to turn the series into his own personal highlight show. But even though he had not played the outfield regularly since 1972, he looked as though he had never missed a game there. He turned in a dazzling defensive performance, making at least one breathtaking play in each game of the series.

In Game 1, Yastrzemski raced to the base of the Green Monster and made a leaping catch of a Billy Williams line drive, never once slowing down to check his distance from the wall. Game 2 saw him throw a strike to third base to nail Bert Campaneris—one of the game's fastest runners—after Sal Bando had ripped a shot off the wall. In Game 3, Yastrzemski robbed Reggie Jackson of an extra base not once but twice.

"I don't think enough people realize what Carl did," Baltimore Orioles manager Earl Weaver said after watching Yastrzemski patrol the outfield. "He didn't just play left field well, he played it like no one has ever played it before. He dominated that series with Oakland. It was incredible to watch a man of his age do what he did without having played there all year."

Yastrzemski also batted .455 and hit a home run, as Boston stunned Oakland by sweeping the series in three games. Almost before anyone knew what had happened, the Oakland A's dynasty was dead, and the Red Sox were headed to the World Series.

The 1975 World Series has gone down in baseball lore as one of the most thrilling ever, but for Yastrzemski and the Red Sox it ended in bitter disappointment. Boston lost to the Cincinnati Reds, four games to three, and each one of the Red Sox' four losses was by a single run.

Yastrzemski batted .310 in the seven-game series to bring his overall World Series batting average to .352, among the highest career marks of all time. Coming on top of his phenomenal performance against Oakland in the playoffs, his exploits cemented his reputation as one of baseball's best clutch players.

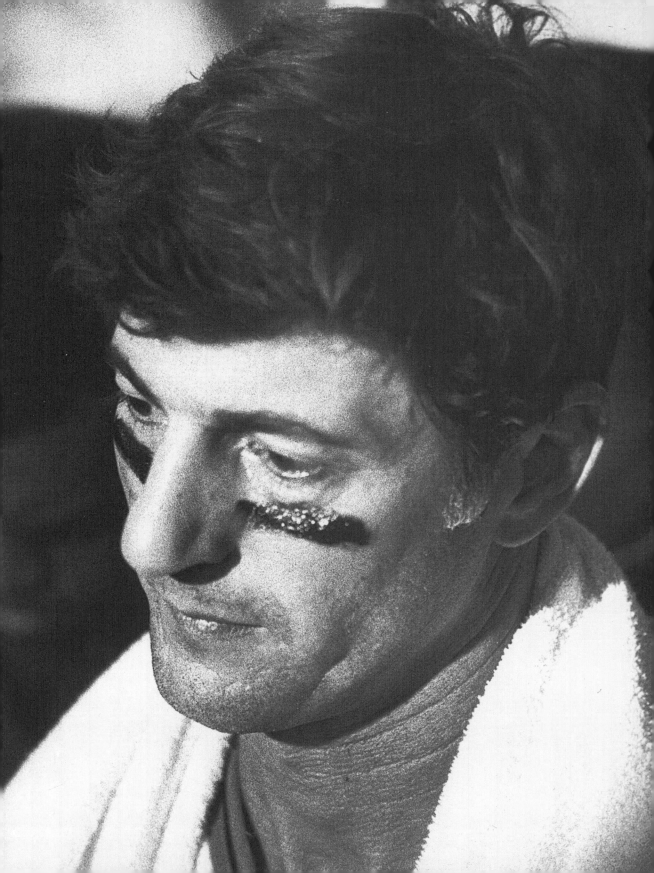

7

A TRUE SUPERSTAR

A bitterly disappointed Yastrzemski reflects on the Red Sox' 5–4 loss to the New York Yankees, moments after the end of their 1978 American League playoff game.

As Carl Yastrzemski entered the latter stages of his playing career, he kept himself in such top shape that between ages 36 to 41 he hit 23 more home runs and collected 41 more runs batted in than he had between ages 21 to 26. On the night of May 19, 1976, he gave the clearest indication that his age was not catching up with him. Playing against the Tigers in Detroit, the 36-year-old star blasted three homers in one game for the first time in his career. The following night, he clubbed two more home runs against the Yankees in New York. His five homers in two games tied the all-time major league record and made him the first American Leaguer to accomplish the feat in 40 years.

Yastrzemski finished the 1976 season with 21 home runs and 102 RBIs, his best totals since 1970. He was even better in 1977: he batted .296 with 28 homers and 102 RBIs while once again playing full-time in left field. He recorded 16 assists that year to lead American League outfielders for a record seventh time, and he did not make a single error all season. At age 38, he won his seventh Gold Glove Award.

The 1977 Red Sox were a powerful team, hitting a whopping 213 home runs on their way to capturing 97 games, more than either the 1967 or 1975 teams had won. Unfortunately, the Yankees won 100 games, and 97 victories was good enough for only a second-place tie in the American League's Eastern Division.

In 1978, Boston again fought New York for the division title. The Red Sox stormed into first place early in the season and threatened to turn the race into a runaway. At one point, they led the Yankees by 14½ games. But New York crept back into contention, and when Boston slumped horridly in early September, the Yankees jumped out to a 3½-game lead with 14 games to play. The Red Sox bounced back, winning 12 of their last 14 games—including 8 straight—to finish their schedule with a 99–63 record, tying New York for first place.

The two teams squared off to determine the Eastern Division winner on Monday afternoon, October 2, in only the second one-game play-off in American League history. Fenway Park was jammed to the rafters, and the hometown crowd cheered wildly when 39-year-old Carl Yastrzemski drove a fastball into the right field seats for a home run and a 1–0 lead off fire-balling Ron Guidry.

Boston pitcher Mike Torrez kept New York at bay through six innings. But a three-run homer by weak-hitting Yankees shortstop Bucky Dent put New York ahead in the seventh inning; Yastrzemski could only watch helplessly as the ball—and the Red Sox' pennant hopes—sailed over the Green Monster.

New York Yankees short-stop Bucky Dent jumps on home plate and is greeted by teammates Roy White (left) and Chris Chambliss (right) after hitting a three-run homer in the seventh inning of the 1978 American League playoff game at Fenway Park.

New York extended its lead to 5–2; then Boston began to battle back. By the bottom of the ninth inning, the Red Sox were trailing by just a single run, 5–4, and had runners poised at the corners with two men out. The entire 1978 season hung in the balance as Yastrzemski stepped into the batters box against the Yankees bullpen ace, Rich ("Goose") Gossage.

In the eighth inning, Yastrzemski had singled off Gossage to make the score 5–3 and had crossed home plate moments later to make it 5–4. This time, however, Gossage got Yastrzemski to hit a pop fly to third baseman Graig Nettles, who snared the ball in foul territory to end Boston's season. Yastrzemski later called his last at-bat in the playoff the greatest disappointment of his career, even more upsetting than having the Red Sox lose the final game of either the 1967 or the 1975 World Series.

Yastrzemski managed to offset his disappointment somewhat in 1979 by becoming the first American Leaguer to amass 400 home runs and 3,000 career base hits. Only three other players had ever reached both milestones: Hank

Yastrzemski watches the flight of his 400th career home run on July 24, 1979, at Fenway Park.

Aaron, Willie Mays, and Yastrzemski's boyhood hero Stan Musial.

Yastrzemski started the 1979 season red-hot and was hitting .306 with 16 homers and 53 RBIs by the end of June. He clouted his 400th career home run on July 24, in a game at Fenway against Oakland Athletics pitcher Mike Morgan. His 3,000th base hit came seven weeks later, in the middle of a terrible batting slump. On September 12 at Fenway Park, after going hitless in his last 13 at-bats, he stepped up to the plate in the eighth inning against Yankees pitcher Jim Beattie and ripped a fastball into right field, just past the lunging second baseman, Willie Randolph.

The game was stopped, and Yastrzemski's family rushed onto the field in celebration as the center-field scoreboard flashed "3,000" over and over. A microphone was set up along the first-base line so the man of the hour could make a brief speech. "I know one thing," Yastrzemski told the crowd, "this one was the hardest of the 3,000. I took so long because I've enjoyed all those standing ovations you've given me the last three days."

After the season, Yastrzemski was honored at the White House by President Jimmy Carter for accomplishing a pair of feats that neither Ty Cobb, Babe Ruth, nor Ted Williams had achieved. But it was the praise from his peers that proved the most satisfying. Perhaps Reggie Jackson, who fielded the 3,000th hit in right field, put it best. "He's a true superstar," Jackson said of Yastrzemski. "It takes a special human to perform at such a level for such a long time."

8

FROM FENWAY TO COOPERSTOWN

With his 400th home run and 3,000th base hit, Carl Yastrzemski assured himself a place alongside baseball's all-time greats. But as the 1980 season began, he was giving little thought to retirement. And by late August, he was batting .275 with 15 home runs. They were respectable numbers for any player but absolutely amazing for a player of Yastrzemski's age.

On August 31, 1980, just nine days after his 41st birthday, Yastrzemski was playing left field as the Boston Red Sox faced the Oakland Athletics at Fenway Park. A's catcher Jim Essian lined a shot toward the Green Monster. Yastrzemski raced back to grab it and crashed into the wall. He held onto the ball, but he also broke one of his ribs and ended his season. The injury also concluded his career as an outfielder. For the remainder of his playing days, he was primarily a designated hitter.

Yastrzemski had a poor year in 1981, but he rebounded in 1982 to bat .275 with 16 home runs and 72 RBIs. To some observers, it must

Yastrzemski gets ready for the 1983 season, his 23rd and final year in the big leagues.

Two of the greatest hitters in Boston Red Sox history, Ted Williams (right) and the man who replaced him in the lineup, Carl Yastrzemski.

have seemed that he would never retire. Yastrzemski could tell that his career was winding down, however, and he wanted to exit gracefully. He did not want to put the Red Sox in the position of having to ask him to retire, or even worse, to release him. So he decided that 1983 would be his final season.

As Boston made its final visit to each American League city that year, Yastrzemski was honored with a seemingly endless series of tributes. The most emotional farewell, of course, took place at Fenway Park. On Saturday, October 1—the regular season's final weekend—the Red Sox honored Yastrzemski with Yaz Day. The occasion was marked by speeches and gifts and tears.

Yastrzemski played his last game the next afternoon, with Boston hosting the Cleveland Indians in the season finale. When he looked at the lineup card before the game, for the final time in his 23-year career, he saw that Manager Ralph Houk had penciled him in as the Red Sox' starting left fielder. He had not played the outfield since breaking a rib three years ago, but he knew that guarding the Green Monster was a fitting way for him to retire.

After the game, in which he recorded the 3,419th hit of his career, Yastrzemski made a final lap around the entire park, waving and shaking hands with as many fans as he possibly could. It was a touching personal gesture from an athlete who had become the most popular player ever to wear a Red Sox uniform. His farewell lap later became one of the great moments in baseball history, featured in the closing credits of the weekly television show "This Week in Baseball."

Many professional athletes find it difficult to adjust to life once their playing days are over. But Yastrzemski, who had earned a bachelor of science degree in business administration from Merrimack College, had always been careful to prepare himself for life after baseball. And because of his careful planning he was able to make the transition from ballplayer to businessman with ease.

For years, Yastrzemski had been doing commercials and promotional work for Kahn's, a meat company. He had also taken the time to learn about the other aspects of the company's business. He attended seminars and visited the company's various plants. By the time he retired from baseball and stepped into a full-time position with Kahn's, he knew the meat business inside out.

Meanwhile, Yastrzemski remained involved with baseball by coaching the Red Sox' young hitters at the ballclub's Winter Haven, Florida, training camp. And in 1989, he was inducted into the Baseball Hall of Fame. His accomplishments as a player spoke for themselves. He had played in 3,308 major league games, a record second only to Pete Rose's total. Yastrzemski was ninth on the all-time RBI list, seventh on the all-time hit list, and fourth all time in bases on balls. In addition, he had won one Triple Crown, one MVP Award, three batting titles, and seven Gold Gloves.

Aside from 1936, when the first group of players were inducted into the Hall of Fame, only 17 players had ever been elected in their first year on the ballot. Despite his splendid career totals, Yastrzemski had not been certain that he would become the 18th.

As it turned out, he had little to worry about. The Baseball Writers of America, who do the voting for the Hall of Fame, cast 447 ballots in Yastrzemski's first year of eligibility. Yastrzemski's name appeared on 423 of them, meaning that 94.6 percent of the writers had voted for him. That summer, he and Johnny Bench entered the Hall of Fame as first-ballot inductees.

The induction ceremony took place on July 23, 1989, in Cooperstown, New York. There Yastrzemski explained how an unspectacular-looking kid from a Long Island potato farm became a Hall of Famer. "I can stand before you today," he said, "and honestly tell you that every day I put on that Red Sox uniform I gave 100 percent of myself. . . . Anything less would not have been worthy of me, anything more would not have been possible."

Induction into the Hall of Fame is the greatest honor any baseball player can receive, but Yastrzemski was given one more tribute during the summer of 1989 that proved just as meaningful. On August 6, the Red Sox retired his uniform number. The ballclub commemorated the occasion by unveiling a large replica of Yastrzemski's number 8 on the facing of Fenway Park's right-field roof, not far from where Ted Williams's uniform number 9 was hung.

Nearly three decades after he had broken into the big leagues, Carl Yastrzemski had emerged from Ted Williams's shadow for good.

CHRONOLOGY

1939	Born Carl Michael Yastrzemski in Southampton, New York, on August 22
1957	Carl Yastrzemski, Sr., advises his son to turn down a $40,000 bonus to sign with the New York Yankees; Carl, Jr., attends the University of Notre Dame
1959	Signs a two-year minor league contract with the Boston Red Sox for $108,000; becomes the Carolina League's most valuable player, with a .377 batting average, 170 hits, 34 doubles, and 15 home runs
1960	Marries Carol Casper in January; sent to Boston's top minor league team, the Minneapolis Millers, to learn to play left field; finishes the season with 193 hits and a .339 batting average
1961	Makes his major league debut with the Boston Red Sox; finishes the season with a .266 batting average, 80 RBIs, and 11 home runs
1962	Leads the league's outfielders with 19 assists; hits .296 with 19 home runs and 94 RBIs
1963	Wins his first American League Batting championship with a .321 average; makes the American League All-Star Team for the first time; heads the league in assists (18) and wins his first of seven Gold Glove Awards
1966	Graduates from Merrimack College
1967	Wins the Triple Crown with a .326 average, 121 RBIs, and 44 home runs; leads Boston to the American League pennant; voted the league's most valuable player and *Sports Illustrated* Sportsman of the Year
1968	Posts a .301 average to win his second consecutive batting championship
1970	Named most valuable player of the All-Star Game; hits .329 for the season, the highest average of his career
1974	Leads the league in runs scored with 93
1975	Leads Boston to a surprising pennant victory over the Oakland Athletics with a .455 average and a home run in the American League Championship Series; makes his second and last appearance in the World Series
1979	Hits his 400th home run on July 24 and records his 3,000th base hit on September 12; becomes the first American Leaguer to amass 400 home runs and 3,000 career base hits
1983	Ends his playing career with 3,308 games played, the most in American League history; honored at Yaz Day at Fenway Park on October 1
1989	Inducted into the Baseball Hall of Fame on July 23; his baseball uniform number, 8, is retired on August 6

CARL MICHAEL YASTRZEMSKI
"YAZ"
BOSTON, A.L., 1961-1983
SUCCEEDED TED WILLIAMS IN FENWAY'S LEFT FIELD
IN 1961 AND RETIRED 23 YEARS LATER AS ALL-TIME
RED SOX LEADER IN 8 CATEGORIES. PLAYED WITH
GRACEFUL INTENSITY IN RECORD 3,308 A.L. GAMES.
ONLY A.L. PLAYER WITH 3,000 HITS AND 400 HOMERS.
3-TIME BATTING CHAMPION. WON MVP AND TRIPLE
CROWN IN 1967 AS HE LED RED SOX TO "IMPOSSIBLE
DREAM" PENNANT.

MAJOR LEAGUE STATISTICS

BOSTON RED SOX

YEAR	TEAM	G	AB	R	H	2B	3B	HR	RBI	BA	SB
1961	BOS A	148	583	71	155	31	6	11	80	.266	6
1962		160	646	99	191	43	6	19	94	.296	7
1963		151	570	91	183	40	3	14	68	.321	8
1964		151	567	77	164	29	9	15	67	.289	6
1965		133	494	78	154	45	3	20	72	.312	7
1966		160	594	81	165	39	2	16	80	.278	8
1967		161	579	112	189	31	4	44	121	.326	10
1968		157	539	90	162	32	2	23	74	.301	13
1969		162	603	96	154	28	2	40	111	.255	15
1970		161	566	125	186	29	0	40	102	.329	23
1971		148	508	75	129	21	2	15	70	.254	8
1972		125	455	70	120	18	2	12	68	.264	5
1973		152	540	82	160	25	4	19	95	.296	9
1974		148	515	93	155	25	2	15	79	.301	12
1975		149	543	91	146	30	1	14	60	.269	8
1976		155	546	71	146	23	2	21	102	.267	5
1977		150	558	99	165	27	3	28	102	.296	11
1978		144	523	70	145	21	2	17	81	.277	4
1979		147	518	69	140	28	1	21	87	.270	3
1980		105	364	49	100	21	1	15	50	.275	0
1981		91	338	36	83	14	1	7	53	.246	0
1982		131	459	53	126	22	1	16	72	.275	0
1983		119	380	38	101	24	0	10	56	.266	0
Totals		3308	11988	1816	3419	646	59	452	1844	.285	168

League Championship Series

		G	AB	R	H	2B	3B	HR	RBI	BA	SB
(1 year)		3	11	4	5	1	0	1	2	.455	0

World Series

		G	AB	R	H	2B	3B	HR	RBI	BA	SB
(2 years)		14	54	11	19	2	0	3	9	.352	0

FURTHER READING

Coleman, Ken, and Dan Valenti. *The Impossible Dream Remembered*. Lexington, MA: The Stephen Greene Press, 1987.

Dickey, Glenn. *The History of American League Baseball*. Briarcliff Manor, NY: Stein and Day, 1980.

Gammons, Peter. "Yastrzemski Recalls His Most Memorable Games." *Baseball Digest*, September 1981.

Ribowsky, Mark. "Patron Saint of the Red Sox." *Sport*, October 1978.

Riley, Dan. *The Red Sox Reader*. Boston: Houghton Mifflin, 1991.

Shatzkin, Mike, and Jim Charlton. *The Ballplayers*. New York: Morrow, 1990.

Wolff, Rick. *Ted Williams*. New York: Chelsea House, 1993.

Yastrzemski, Carl, and Gerald Eskenazi. *Yaz: Baseball, The Wall and Me*. New York: Doubleday, 1990.

INDEX

PICTURE CREDITS

AP/Wide World Photos: p. 54; AP/Wide World Photo, Print courtesy National Baseball Library, Cooperstown, NY: p. 11; Courtesy the Bridgehampton Historical Society: pp. 14, 16; National Baseball Library, Cooperstown, NY: p. 60; The University of Notre Dame Archive: p. 20; UPI/Bettmann: pp. 2, 8, 23, 26, 28, 30, 32, 34, 35, 36, 38, 40, 43, 44, 46, 49, 50, 52, 58

SHEPARD LONG is a researcher and writer for the Phoenix Communications Group, the official television production company of both Major League Baseball and the National Hockey League. His television writing credits include "Baseball '91," "Power Stick Hockey Week," and the home-video series *Play Ball the Major League Way*. He is also on the staff of the syndicated television series "This Week in Baseball," and contributed extensively to both *The Ballplayers* and *The Baseball Chronology*. He and his wife Patricia live in Hoboken, New Jersey, the birthplace of baseball.

JIM MURRAY, veteran sports columnist of the *Los Angeles Times*, is one of America's most acclaimed writers. He has been named "America's Best Sportswriter" by the National Association of Sportscasters and Sportswriters 14 times, was awarded the Red Smith Award, and was twice winner of the National Headliner Award. In addition, he was awarded the J. G. Taylor Spink Award in 1987 for "meritorious contributions to baseball writing." With this award came his 1988 induction into the National Baseball Hall of Fame in Cooperstown, New York. In 1990, Jim Murray was awarded the Pulitzer Prize for Commentary.

EARL WEAVER is the winningest manager in Baltimore Orioles history by a wide margin. He compiled 1,480 victories in his 17 years at the helm. After managing eight different minor league teams, he was given the chance to lead the Orioles in 1968. Under his leadership the Orioles finished lower than second place in the American League East only four times in 17 years. One of only 12 managers in big league history to have managed in four or more World Series, Earl was named Manager of the Year in 1979. The popular Weaver had his number 5 retired in 1982, joining Brooks Robinson, Frank Robinson, and Jim Palmer, whose numbers were retired previously. Earl Weaver continues his association with the professional baseball scene by writing, broadcasting, and coaching.